Congressional Research Service

Drought in the United States: Causes and Issues for Congress

Peter Folger
Specialist in Energy and Natural Resources Policy

Betsy A. Cody
Specialist in Natural Resources Policy

Nicole T. Carter
Specialist in Natural Resources Policy

June 12, 2012

Congressional Research Service
7-5700
www.crs.gov
RL34580

CRS Report for Congress ————————————————
Prepared for Members and Committees of Congress

Summary

Drought is a natural hazard with potentially significant societal, economic, and environmental consequences. Public policy issues related to drought range from how to identify and measure drought to how best to prepare for, respond to, and mitigate drought impacts, and who should bear such costs. This report provides information relevant to drought policy discussions by describing the physical causes of drought, drought history in the United States, examples of regional drought conditions, and policy challenges related to drought.

What is drought? Drought is commonly defined as a lack of precipitation over an extended period of time, usually a season or more, relative to some long-term average condition. While the technology and science to predict droughts have improved, regional predictions remain limited to a few months in advance. History suggests that severe and extended droughts are inevitable and part of natural climate cycles.

What causes drought? The physical conditions causing drought in the United States are increasingly understood to be linked to sea surface temperatures (SSTs) in the tropical Pacific Ocean. Studies indicate that cooler-than-average SSTs have been connected to the severe western drought in the first decade of the 21st century, severe droughts of the late 19th century, and precolonial North American "megadroughts." The 2011 severe drought in Texas is thought to be linked to La Niña conditions in the Pacific Ocean.

What is the future of drought in the United States? The prospect of extended droughts and more arid baseline conditions in parts of the United States could suggest new challenges to federal water projects, which were constructed largely on the basis of 20th century climate conditions. Some studies suggest that the American West may be transitioning to a more arid climate, possibly resulting from the buildup of greenhouse gases in the atmosphere, raising concerns that the region may become more prone to extreme drought it was in the 20th century. Some models of future climate conditions also predict greater fluctuations in wet and dry years.

California's 2007-2009 drought exacerbated ongoing tensions among competing water uses. While drought is most common in California and the Southwest, drought also can exacerbate water tensions in other regions. For example, the 2007-2008 drought in the Southeast heightened a long-standing dispute in the Apalachicola-Chattahoochee-Flint River (ACF) basin. Both California and the ACF are again experiencing drought conditions, as are the Rio Grande and Upper Colorado River basins.

What are some drought policy challenges? Although the impacts of drought can be significant nationally as well as regionally, comprehensive national drought policy does not exist. Developing such a policy would represent a significant challenge because of split federal and non-federal responsibilities, the existing patchwork of federal drought programs, and differences in regional conditions and risks. While a comprehensive national policy has not been enacted, Congress has considered and acted upon some of the recommendations issued by the National Drought Policy Commission in 2000. In coming years, Congress may review how federal agencies such as the U.S. Army Corps of Engineers and the Bureau of Reclamation respond to droughts. Congress may also assess other federal programs or choose to reassess the National Drought Policy Commission's recommendations.

Contents

Figures

Appendixes

Contacts

Introduction

The likelihood of extended periods of severe drought, similar to conditions experienced centuries ago, and its effects on 21st century society in the United States raise several issues for Congress. Drought often results in significant agricultural losses, which can have widespread effects. It also can impact other industries and services, including power and energy resource production, navigation, recreation, municipal water supplies, and natural resources such as fisheries and water quality. Addressing drought impacts on an emergency basis is costly to individuals, communities, and businesses. Additionally, hundreds of millions and sometimes billions of dollars in federal assistance can be expended in attempting to manage drought's social consequences.

Drought has afflicted portions of North America for thousands of years. Severe, long-lasting droughts may have been a factor in the disintegration of Pueblo society in the Southwest during the 13th century, and in the demise of central and lower Mississippi Valley societies in the 14th through 16th centuries.[1] In the 20th century, droughts in the 1930s (Dust Bowl era) and 1950s were particularly severe and widespread. In 1934, 65% of the contiguous United States was affected by severe to extreme drought.[2]

Drought conditions are broadly grouped into five categories: (1) abnormally dry, (2) moderate, (3) severe, (4) extreme, and (5) exceptional.[3] Some part of the country is almost always experiencing drought at some level. Since 2000, no less than 7% of the land area of the United States has experienced drought of at least moderate intensity each year.[4] The land area affected by drought of at least moderate intensity varies by year and also within a particular year. For example, since 2000, the total U.S. land area affected by drought of at least moderate intensity has varied from as little as 7% (August 3, 2010) to as much as 46% (September 10, 2002). Based on weekly estimates of the areal extent of drought conditions since 2000, the average amount of land area across the United States affected by at least moderate-intensity drought has been 25%.

While the previous percentages refer to the extent of drought nationally, there is particular concern about those locations experiencing the most intense drought conditions. Nearly every year, *extreme drought*[5] affects some portion of the country. Since 2000, extreme drought or drier conditions have affected approximately 6% of the nation on average.[6] During August 2002, extreme drought extended over 19% of the country. Since 2000, *exceptional drought* conditions have affected approximately 1% of the nation on average. Of particular note were the conditions

---

[1] Edward R. Cook, Richard Seager, Mark A. Crane, and David W. Stahle, "North American drought: reconstructions, causes, and consequences," *Earth-Science Reviews*, vol. 81 (2007): pp. 93-134. Hereafter referred to as Cook et al., 2007.

[2] Donald A. Wilhite, et al., *Managing Drought A Roadmap for Change in the United States* (Boulder, CO: The Geological Society of America, 2007), p. 12; at http://www.geosociety.org/meetings/06drought/roadmap.pdf.

[3] These are the categories used by the National Drought Mitigation Center (NDMC). The NDMC helps prepare the U.S. Drought Monitor and maintains its website.

[4] NDMC data collected since 2000. U.S. Drought Monitor at the NDMC in Lincoln, NE. See http://droughtmonitor.unl.edu/dmtabs_archive.htm.

[5] Extreme drought is the fourth of five categories indicating drought conditions, ranging from abnormally dry to exceptional drought, according to the National Drought Mitigation Center.

[6] In some years or months, however, no part of the country was under extreme or exceptional drought. For example, from January 2000 through early April 2000, extreme or exceptional drought did not affect any portion of the country.

---

between June and October 2011; exceptional drought occurred over the largest land area—greater than 9%—during those months, with the affected areas concentrated in Texas.

This report discusses how drought is defined (e.g., why drought in one region of the country is different from drought in another region), and why drought occurs in the United States. How droughts are classified, and what is meant by moderate, severe, and extreme drought classifications, are also discussed. The report briefly describes periods of drought in the country's past that equaled or exceeded drought conditions experienced during the 20th century. This is followed by a discussion of the future prospects for a climate in the West that would be drier than the average 20th-century climate. The report concludes with a primer on policy challenges for Congress, such as the existing federal/non-federal split in drought response and management and the patchwork of drought programs subject to oversight by multiple congressional committees. An exhaustive discussion of each policy challenge facing Congress is beyond the scope of this report.

What Is Drought?

Drought has a number of definitions; the simplest may be a deficiency of precipitation over an extended period of time, usually a season or more.[7] Drought is usually considered relative to some long-term average condition, or balance, between precipitation, evaporation, and transpiration by plants (evaporation and transpiration are typically combined into one term: evapotranspiration).[8] An imbalance could result from a decrease in precipitation, an increase in evapotranspiration (from drier conditions, higher temperatures, higher winds), or both. It is important to distinguish between drought, which has a beginning and an end, and aridity, which is restricted to low rainfall regions and is a relatively permanent feature of climate (e.g., deserts are regions of relatively permanent aridity).[9]

Higher demand for water for human activities and vegetation in areas of limited water supply increases the severity of drought. For example, drought during the growing season would likely be considered more severe—in terms of its impacts—than similar conditions when cropland lies fallow. For policy purposes, drought often becomes an issue when it results in a water supply deficiency: Less water is available than the average amount for irrigation, municipal and industrial supply (M&I), energy production, preservation of endangered species, and other needs. At the national level, drought is monitored and reported by the National Drought Mitigation Center in an index known as the U.S. Drought Monitor, which synthesizes various drought indices and impacts, and represents a consensus view of ongoing drought conditions between academic and federal scientists.

Drought Is Relative

Drought and "normal" conditions can vary considerably from region to region. For example, in May 2012, the cities of Lubbock, TX, and Athens, GA, were within areas of extreme drought,

---

[7] NDMC, http://www.drought.unl.edu/DroughtBasics/WhatisDrought.aspx.

[8] Evapotranspiration may be defined as the loss of water from a land area through transpiration from plants and evaporation from the soil and surface water bodies such as lakes, ponds, and manmade reservoirs.

[9] Permanently arid conditions reflect the *climate* of the region, which is the composite of the day-to-day weather over a longer period of time. Climatologists traditionally interpret climate as the 30-year average. See NDMC, http://www.drought.unl.edu/DroughtBasics/WhatisClimatology.aspx.

---

according to the U.S. Drought Monitor.[10] (See **Figure 1**.) However, extreme drought means something different to Lubbock, in northwest Texas, than it does for Athens, in north central Georgia. Lubbock receives an average total of 3.26 inches of precipitation for the three-month period from February through April of each year.[11] In contrast, Athens receives an average of 12.06 inches over the same time period.[12] From February 2012 through April 2012, Athens received 6.03 inches, which equates to 1.85 times the average precipitation normally received in Lubbock over that time period, but is only 50% of what Athens receives on average. Both cities faced extreme drought compared to normal conditions, but what defines normal for each city differs substantially.

To deal with these differences, meteorologists use the term meteorological drought—usually defined as the degree of dryness relative to some average amount of dryness and relative to the duration of the dry period. Meteorological drought is region-specific because atmospheric conditions creating precipitation deficiencies vary from region to region, as described above for Lubbock and Athens.

Figure 1. Extent of Drought in the United States on May 8, 2012

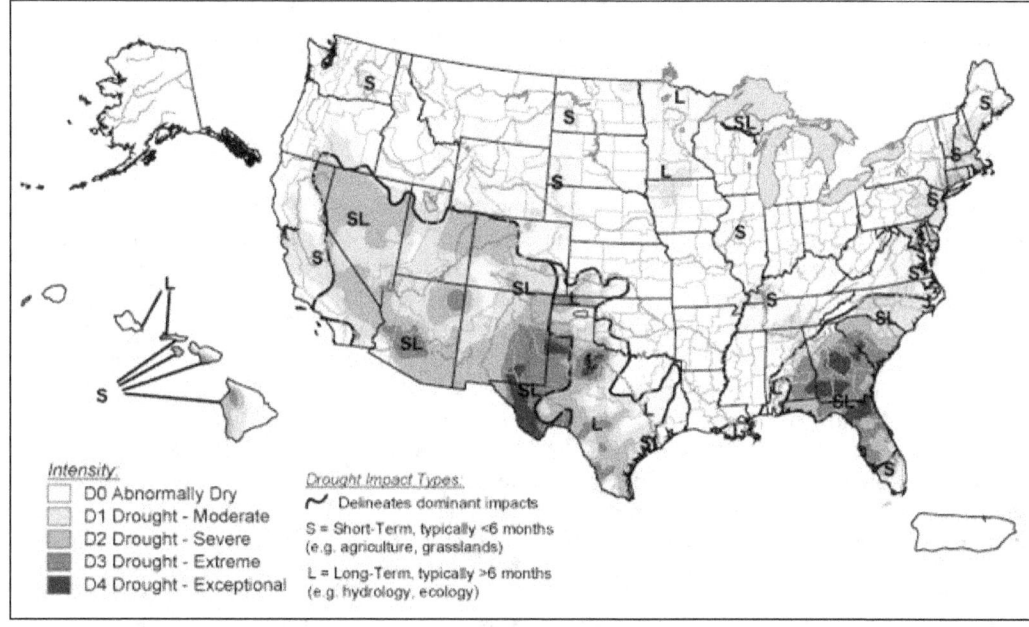

Source: U.S. Drought Monitor, at http://droughtmonitor.unl.edu/, May 8, 2012. Modified by CRS.

Note: The areas delineated on the map as "drought impact types" depict regions where reports of specific impacts (e.g., short term (S) or long term (L) impacts) have been reported and tallied. For more information, see http://www.cpc.ncep.noaa.gov/products/predictions/tools/edb/droughtblends.php.

---

[10] See U.S. Drought Monitor, http://www.drought.unl.edu/dm/monitor.html.

[11] The National Weather Service Forecast Office, Lubbock, Texas, http://www.weather.gov/climate/index.php?wfo=lub.

[12] The National Weather Service Forecast Office, Peachtree City, GA, http://www.nws.noaa.gov/climate/index.php?wfo=ffc.

Drought Is Multifaceted

In the past, U.S. Drought Monitor maps have used an "A" to indicate that the primary physical effects are agricultural (crops, pastures, and grasslands) and an "H" to indicate that the primary impacts of drought are hydrological (to water supplies such as rivers, groundwater, and reservoirs). When both effects are apparent, the letters are combined, appearing as "AH." In the newer versions of the maps, such as the one shown in **Figure 1**, the "A" and "H" are replaced with an "S" and "L." These are experimental designations, according to the National Drought Mitigation Center, which produces the U.S. Drought Monitor maps.[13] The "S" designation is intended to indicate a combination of drought indices that reflect impacts that respond to precipitation over several days up to a few months (short-term effects). These would include impact to agriculture, topsoil moisture, unregulated streamflows, and aspects of wildfire danger. The "L" designation approximates responses to precipitation over several months up to a few years (long-term effects). These would include reservoir levels, groundwater, and lake levels. **Figure 1** shows that the region around Lubbock, TX, is designated as L, whereas the region closest to Athens, GA, shows an SL, indicating a combination of short-term and long-term effects.

The U.S. Drought Monitor maps also indicate the intensity of a drought, ranging from abnormally dry (shown as D0 on the maps) to exceptional drought (shown as D4). How these conditions are assessed and how drought is classified are discussed below.

Drought Classification

To assess and classify the intensity and type of drought, certain measures, or drought indices, are typically used. Drought intensity, in turn, is the trigger for local, state, and federal responses that can lead to the flow of billions of dollars in relief to drought-stricken regions.[14] The classification of drought intensity, such as that shown in **Figure 1** for May 8, 2012, may depend on a single indicator or several indicators, often combined with expert opinion from the academic, public, and private sectors. The U.S. Drought Monitor uses five key indicators,[15] together with expert opinion, with indices to account for conditions in the West where snowpack is relatively important, and with other indices used mainly during the growing season.[16] The U.S. Drought Monitor intensity scheme—D0 to D4—is used to depict broad-scale conditions but not necessarily drought circumstances at the local scale. For example, the large regions depicted as red in **Figure 1** faced extreme to exceptional drought conditions in May 2012, but they may contain local areas and individual communities that experienced less (or more) severe drought.[17]

---

[13] The complete designations are referred to as experimental objective blends of drought indicators, http://www.cpc.ncep.noaa.gov/products/predictions/tools/edb/droughtblends.php.

[14] For example, the Palmer Drought Index has been widely used by the U.S. Department of Agriculture to determine when to grant emergency drought assistance. See NDMC, http://drought.unl.edu/Planning/Monitoring/ComparisonofIndicesIntro/PDSI.aspx.

[15] The five key indicators include the Palmer Drought Index, the Climate Prediction Center soil moisture model, U.S. Geological Survey weekly streamflow data, the Standardized Precipitation Index, and short- and long-term drought indicator blends. For a discussion of drought indices, see NDMC, http://droughtmonitor.unl.edu/current.html.

[16] U.S. Drought Monitor, http://www.drought.unl.edu/dm/classify.htm.

[17] The "S" and "L" terms shown in **Figure 1** give additional information on the nature of the drought in the affected region. For more information on the reasoning behind the classification schemes, see http://droughtmonitor.unl.edu/classify.htm.

Recent Examples: Texas, California, and Upper Colorado River Basin

Drought in Texas—2011 and 2012

In early May of 2011 over 80% of Texas was experiencing extreme drought, and nearly 50% of the state was in exceptional drought, the most severe level of drought intensity published by the National Drought Mitigation Center.[18] The 2011 drought in Texas represented a dramatic shift compared to the same time period in 2010, when less than 6% of the total land area in Texas was experiencing drought conditions, with no exceptional drought conditions anywhere in the state. (See **Figure 2**, comparing 2010, 2011, and 2012.) In May 2012 the eastern half of Texas had recovered from extreme or exceptional conditions, which—as of May 8, 2012—were affecting 24% and 7% of the state, respectively.

Figure 2. Comparison of Drought Conditions in Texas in 2010, 2011, and 2012

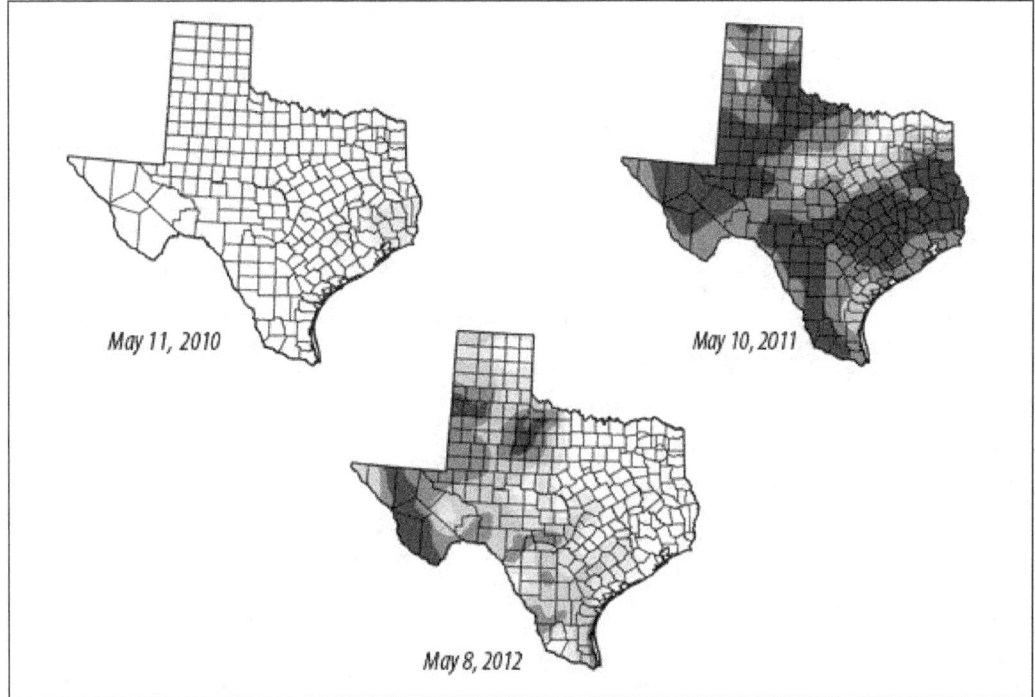

May 11, 2010

May 10, 2011

May 8, 2012

Source: U.S. Drought Monitor, http://droughtmonitor.unl.edu/, Modified by CRS.

Drought conditions worsened in Texas through the beginning of October 2011, when 88% of the state experienced exceptional drought conditions (and only 3% of the state was not classified as extreme or exceptional drought).[19] Drought conditions generally improved throughout the rest of 2011, but large portions of the state were still affected by extreme or exceptional drought until

---

[18] U.S. Drought Monitor, http://droughtmonitor.unl.edu/dmtabs_archive.htm.

[19] See the U.S. Drought Monitor, Texas, on October 4, 2011, http://droughtmonitor.unl.edu/archive.html.

late winter and early spring of 2012, when the eastern portion of the state recovered to normal or abnormally dry conditions (the least severe category) because of above-normal rainfall from December 2011 through February 2012.[20]

Drought Conditions Affecting the Rio Grande Project in 2011 and 2012

The 2011 and 2012 drought conditions in Texas and the Southwest have affected the amount of water in the Rio Grande river, which flows south through New Mexico to form the U.S. border between Texas and northern Mexico. The U.S. Bureau of Reclamation's Rio Grande Project, which furnishes irrigation water for approximately 178,000 acres in New Mexico and Texas, as well as electric power, includes the Elephant Butte dam and reservoir and the Caballo Dam and reservoir. Both dams and reservoirs are in New Mexico, and about 60% of the lands receiving irrigation water are in New Mexico. Elephant Butte dam and reservoir provide year-round electric power generation and water during the irrigation season. Water released from Elephant Butte during winter power generation is stored downstream in the Caballo reservoir for irrigation use during the summer. About 40% of the lands receiving water from the project are in Texas, and water is also provided for diversion to Mexico to irrigate about 25,000 acres in the Juarez Valley. The timing of the water releases in 2012 for delivery to Mexico and their potential impacts on U.S. regional interests (e.g., potential conveyance losses because releases for Mexico would not be timed with deliveries to U.S. water districts) have raised some concerns among some U.S. stakeholders about how scarce regional water resources are to be managed during these dry conditions. Mexican growers sought the surface water deliveries because pumping problems had impaired their ability to start the agricultural season using groundwater.

Inflow to Elephant Butte reservoir in 2011 was less than 15% of the 30-year average for March through July and is expected to be 23% for 2012. The 2011 drought exacerbated low flows into the reservoir; flows into the reservoir have exceeded average runoff values only three times in the past 15 years (1997, 2005, and 2008). As a result, the Elephant Butte reservoir was at 9.6% of the combined reservoir capacity of 2.23 million acre-feet in early September 2011. For April 2012, it was at 17.9% of capacity. Consequently, the average water allocation from the Rio Grande Project in 2011 was approximately 43% (although water available to individual water districts varies). The 2012 allocation is projected to be 20.5%, due to cumulative low inflows in the reservoirs. In contrast, the average allocation in 2009 was 100%.

Due to low water levels, water deliveries from the Rio Grande Project to the irrigation district in Texas (El Paso County Water Improvement District No. 1) as well as to the city of El Paso ended on September 10, 2011. Under a full allocation, the water deliveries normally extend through mid- or late-October. Because of 2011 conditions, the New Mexico portion of the project, operated by the Elephant Butte Irrigation District, stopped taking surface water deliveries in mid-July 2011. Rio Grande Project water users were receiving a 20% allocation of water supplies as of April 1, 2012.

Sources: U.S. Bureau of Reclamation, Rio Grande Project, http://www.usbr.gov/projects/Project.jsp?proj_Name= Rio+Grande+Project; Texas Agrilife Research Center at El Paso, "Drought Watch on the Rio Grande," September 2, 2011, and May 1, 2012; email from Dionne Thompson, Chief, Congressional and Legislative Affairs, U.S. Bureau of Reclamation, September 15, 2011; personal communication with Fi iberto Cortez, Division Manager, El Paso Field Office, U.S. Bureau of Reclamation, May 2, 2012; letter from Patrick R. Gordon, Texas Commissioner, Rio Grande Compact Commission, to Edward Drusina, Commissioner, United States Section, International Boundary and Water Commission, April 9, 2012.

According to Texas state climatologist John Nielsen-Gammon, 2011 may be the worst one-year drought on record for Texas.[21] Compounding the effects of abnormally low precipitation, the June-August average temperature in Texas was approximately 2.5 degrees Fahrenheit greater than any previous Texas summer since 1895 and 5 degrees Fahrenheit (F) greater than the long-term average.[22] The 2011 U.S. Drought Monitor showed that Texas had been experiencing both

---

[20] "Climate Abyss: Weather and Climate Issues with John Nielsen-Gammon," *Texas Drought Update*, March 23, 2012, http://blog.chron.com/climateabyss/2012/03/texas-drought-update/.

[21] Office of the Texas State Climatologist, "Texas Drought Officially the Worst Ever," August 4, 2011, http://tamunews.tamu.edu/2011/08/04/texas-drought-officially-the-worst-ever/.

[22] John W. Nielsen-Gammon, *The 2011 Texas Drought A Briefing Packet for the Texas Legislature*, October 31, 2011, (continued...)

hydrological and agricultural drought, indicating that the drought has caused deficiencies in water supplies as well as deficiencies of water to crops, plants, and grasses.

The most severe Texas drought overall occurred from 1950 to 1957, and had substantial impacts on water supplies across the state because it lasted over many years. Because of the longevity and severity of the 1950s drought, municipal water supplies in Texas today are designed to withstand a drought of similar magnitude, according to the state climatologist.[23] It is difficult to predict whether drought conditions in Texas will persist through 2012 and longer. Long-term precipitation patterns in Texas are influenced by a configuration of sea surface temperatures known as the Pacific Decadal Oscillation (PDO). According to the Texas state climatologist, the current PDO configuration associated with relatively dry weather in Texas has been present since 1998.[24] Similar conditions also prevailed from the 1940s through the 1960s, encompassing the Texas drought of record (1950-1957).

The 2007-2009 California Drought and Outlook for 2012

The 2007-2009 California drought[25] was complicated by decades of tension over water supply deliveries for irrigation and M&I uses, and the preservation of water flows to protect threatened and endangered species. Dry conditions that began in 2007 continued through the 2009 water year (October 2008 through September 2009) and into the fall of 2009. According to the California Department of Water Resources, the 2007-2009 drought was the 12th-driest three-year period in California history since measurements began.[26] Although hydrological conditions were classified as below normal in 2010 and "wet" (well above average) in 2011, the 2012 water year is projected to be "dry" (well below normal).[27] Above-average reservoir storage at the end of 2011 will mitigate reductions to water users; even so, water deliveries to state and federal water project contractors have been restricted for 2012.[28]

During the drought years, drought conditions changed in the state so that some parts of the state experienced more intense drought than others at different times of the year. For example, spring rains reduced the intensity of the drought in some areas—parts of the state classified as extreme in January 2009 were classified as severe in the late spring of that year. Nearly all of California was classified as abnormally dry or under drought conditions through the fall of 2009 until rain and snow in the late fall and early winter of 2010 relieved drought conditions in parts of the state, including the Sierra Nevada. On March 30, 2011, Governor Jerry Brown proclaimed that the

---

(...continued)

p. 29, http://climatexas.tamu.edu/files/2011_drought.pdf.

[23] Office of the Texas State Climatologist, "Texas Drought Officially the Worst Ever," August 4, 2011, http://tamunews.tamu.edu/2011/08/04/texas-drought-officially-the-worst-ever/.

[24] John W. Nielsen-Gammon, The *2011 Texas Drought A Briefing Packet for the Texas Legislature*, p. 41.

[25] For more information about the hydrology and policy issues involved in the 2007-2009 California drought, see CRS Report R40979, *California Drought Hydrological and Regulatory Water Supply Issues*, by Betsy A. Cody, Peter Folger, and Cynthia Brougher.

[26] California Department of Water Resources, *California's Drought of 2007-2009—An Overview*, September 2010, http://www.water.ca.gov/waterconditions/drought/docs/DroughtReport2010.pdf.

[27] For information on water year classifications and water allocations to federal water contractors in California, see http://www.usbr.gov/mp/PA/water/.

[28] Ibid.

drought was over.[29] Most of California remained drought-free from spring 2010 through December 2011—although the winter precipitation in 2011 was abnormally low. The 2012 Drought Monitor shows moderate drought conditions for most of California's Central Valley from January 2012 through April 2012.

California's dry conditions from 2007 through 2009 exacerbated an already tight water supply, where federal and state water deliveries had been reduced in response to a court order to prevent extinction of the Delta smelt.[30] Governor Arnold Schwarzenegger's decision to declare drought in 2008 reflected the meteorological constraints on water supply together with court-imposed restrictions on water supplies to protect endangered species, and long-standing restrictions to protect water quality in the Delta. This combination of factors underscores why drought is complex and not always simply a result of dry conditions.

Similar factors are still in play today. Water deliveries from state and federal water projects for 2012 are restricted due to legal actions to protect threatened and endangered species, water quality requirements, and hydrological factors. (For more information on project water deliveries, see CRS Report R40979, *California Drought: Hydrological and Regulatory Water Supply Issues* , by Betsy A. Cody, Peter Folger, and Cynthia Brougher

The 2012 Conditions in the Upper Colorado River Basin

Spanning parts of Arizona, California, Colorado, New Mexico, Nevada, Utah, and Wyoming, the Colorado River basin is a critical water supply for the West and portions of northwestern Mexico. Based on inflows observed over the last century, the river is over-allocated, and some contend that supply and demand imbalances are likely to increase in the future.[31] Drought in part of the basin, particularly the upper basin, which is the source of most of the river's flow, exacerbates tensions over the sharing of the resource and results in difficult tradeoffs among the multiple uses of water (e.g., municipal, agricultural, hydropower, energy, recreation, and ecosystem and species demands). How water resources are allocated among these uses within a state is largely determined by state water law, compliance with federal and state laws (including environmental and resource management laws and regulations), and court decisions.

According to the U.S. Drought Monitor, severe drought continued through April 2012 in the Upper Colorado River basin.[32] Although 2011 was a wet water year, upper basin snowpack over the 2011-2012 winter was low,[33] and the snow melted early in the runoff season—one month earlier than normal due to high temperatures in March and April.[34] This early runoff, combined

---

[29] Office of Governor Edmund G. Brown, Jr., "A Proclamation by the Governor of the State of California—Drought," http://gov.ca.gov/news.php?id=16997.

[30] The Delta smelt is a species of fish. *Natural Resources Defense Council v. Kempthorne*, No. 1:05-cv-1207 OWW GSA (E.D. Cal., December 14, 2007).

[31] Bureau of Reclamation, U.S. Department of the Interior, *Colorado River Basin Water Supply and Demand Study, Phase 4 Development and Evaluation of Opportunities for Balancing Water Supply and Demand*, November 2011, http://www.usbr.gov/lc/region/programs/crbstudy/OptionsSubmittalReport.pdf.

[32] National Weather Service, *Drought Information Statement—Denver/Boulder, CO*, May 3, 2012, http://www.srh.noaa.gov/productview.php?pil=DGTBOU.

[33] Natural Resources Conservation Service, U.S. Department of Agriculture, *Westwide Snotel Current Snow Water Equivalent (SWE) % of Normal*, May 1, 2012, http://ccc.atmos.colostate.edu/pdfs/NIDIS_01_May_2012.pdf.

[34] Letter from Water Resources Group, Bureau of Reclamation to All Colorado River Annual Operation Plan (AOP) Recipients, April 24-Month Study, April 10, 2012, http://www.usbr.gov/uc/water/crsp/studies/24Month_04.pdf. (continued...)

---

with high reservoir levels carried over from 2011, produced a somewhat paradoxical situation of combined storage in upper basin reservoirs of 127% of average in April 2012,[35] while inflows to the reservoirs are projected to be well below normal. The worries over future conditions are derived from the exceptionally low streamflows projected for the upper basin[36] because of the poor snowpack; low streamflows mean less inflow into reservoirs over the late spring and summer season.[37] Low water availability in the Upper Colorado basin has effects beyond the basin boundaries. For example, Colorado River water is transported from Colorado's Western Slope to the state's Front Range; this water represents a significant contribution to the water available for agricultural and municipal uses in many eastern Colorado counties.

What Causes Drought in the United States?

The immediate cause of drought is:

> the predominant sinking motion of air (subsidence) that results in compressional warming or high pressure, which inhibits cloud formation and results in lower relative humidity and less precipitation. Regions under the influence of semi permanent high pressure during all or a major portion of the year are usually deserts, such as the Sahara and Kalahari deserts of Africa and the Gobi Desert of Asia.[38]

Prolonged droughts occur when these atmospheric conditions persist for months or years over a certain region that typically does not experience such conditions for a prolonged period.[39]

Predicting drought is difficult because the ability to forecast surface temperature and precipitation depends on a number of key variables, such as air-sea interactions, topography, soil moisture, land surface processes, and other weather system dynamics.[40] Scientists seek to understand how all these variables interact and to further the ability to predict sustained and severe droughts beyond a season or two in advance, which is the limit of drought forecasting abilities today.

In the tropics, a major portion of the atmospheric variability over months or years seems to be associated with variations in sea surface temperatures (SSTs). Since the mid- to late 1990s, scientists have increasingly linked drought in the United States to SSTs in the tropical Pacific Ocean. Cooler than average SSTs in the eastern tropical Pacific region—"la Niña-like" conditions—have been shown to be correlated with persistently strong drought conditions over parts of the country, particularly the West.[41] A number of recent studies have made the connection

---

(...continued)

Hereafter Water Resources Group, April 10, 2012.

[35] Ibid. High inflows in spring and summer of 2011 improved storage levels at basin reservoirs; for instance, Lake Powell increased its storage from 53% in 2010 to 64% in 2011.

[36] Natural Resources Conservation Service, U.S. Department of Agriculture, *Spring and Summer Streamflow Forecasts as of May 1, 2012*, http://www.wcc.nrcs.usda.gov/ftpref/support/water/westwide/streamflow/wy2012/strm1205.gif.

[37] Water Resources Group, April 10, 2012.

[38] See NDMC, at http://drought.unl.edu/DroughtBasics/PredictingDrought.aspx.

[39] Ibid.

[40] Ibid.

[41] Cook et al., 2007.

---

between cooler SSTs in the eastern Pacific and the 1998-2004 western drought,[42] three widespread and persistent droughts of the late 19th century,[43] and past North American "megadroughts" that occurred between approximately 900 and 1300 A.D.[44] The precolonial megadroughts apparently lasted longer and were more extreme than any U.S. droughts since 1850, when instrumental records began. Some modeling studies suggest that within a few decades the western United States may again face higher base levels of dryness, or aridity, akin to the 900-1300 A.D. period.[45]

Although the relationship between cooler than normal eastern tropical Pacific SSTs (La Niña-like conditions) and drought is becoming more firmly established, meteorological drought is probably never the result of a single cause. Climate is inherently variable, and accurately predicting drought for one region in the United States for more than a few months or seasons in advance is not yet possible because so many factors influence regional drought. What is emerging from the scientific study of drought is an improved understanding of global linkages—called teleconnections by scientists—between interacting weather systems, such as the El Niño-Southern Oscillation, or ENSO. (See box for a description of ENSO.) For example, some scientists link La Niña conditions between 1998 and 2002 with the occurrence of near-simultaneous drought in the southern United States, Southern Europe, and Southwest Asia.[46]

El Niño-Southern Oscillation (ENSO)

Under normal conditions, the trade winds blow toward the west in the tropical Pacific Ocean, pi ing up the warm surface waters so that the ocean surface off Indonesia is one-half meter higher than the ocean off Ecuador. As a result, deep and cold water flows up to the surface (upwelling) off the west coast of South America. The upwelling waters are 8 degrees Celsius (14.4 degrees Fahrenheit) cooler than waters in the western Pacific. During El Niño, the trade winds relax, upwelling off South America weakens, and sea surface temperatures rise. The El Niño events occur irregularly at intervals of 2-7 years, and typically last 12-18 months. These events often occur with changes in the Southern Oscillation, a see-saw of atmospheric pressure measured at sea level between the western Pacific and Indian Ocean, and the eastern Pacific. Under normal conditions, atmospheric pressure at sea level is high in the eastern Pacific, and low in the western Pacific and Indian Oceans. As implied by its name, the atmospheric pressure oscillates, or see-saws, between east and west; and during El Niño the atmospheric pressure builds up to abnormally high levels in the western tropical Pacific and Indian Oceans—the El Niño-Southern Oscillation, or ENSO. During a La Niña, the situation is reversed: Abnormally high pressure builds up over the eastern Pacific, the trade winds are abnormally strong, and cooler-than-normal sea surface temperatures occur off tropical South America. Scientists use the terms ENSO or ENSO cycle to include the full range of variability observed, including both El Niño and La Niña events.

Source: Tropical Ocean Atmosphere Project, Pacific Marine Environmental Laboratory, at http://www.pmel.noaa.gov/tao/proj_over/ensodefs.html.

---

[42] Hoerling, Martin and Arun Kumar, "The perfect ocean for drought," *Science*, vol. 299 (January 31, 2003), pp. 691-694. Hereafter referred to as Hoerling and Kumar, 2003.

[43] Herweiger, Celine, Richard Seager, and Edward Cook, "North American droughts of the mid to late nineteenth century: a history, simulation and implication for Mediaeval drought," *The Holocene*, vol. 15, no. 2 (January 31, 2006), pp. 159-171. Hereafter referred to as Herweiger et al., 2006.

[44] Cook et al., 2007.

[45] Richard Seager et al., "Model projections of an imminent transition to a more arid climate in southwestern North America," *Science*, vol. 316 (May 25, 2007): pp. 1181-1184.

[46] Hoerling and Kumar, 2003.

Prehistorical and Historical Droughts in the United States

Some scientists refer to severe drought as "the greatest recurring natural disaster to strike North America."[47] That claim stems from a reconstruction of drought conditions that extends back over 1,000 years, based on observations, historical and instrumental records where available, and on tree-ring records or other proxies in the absence of direct measurements.[48] What these reconstructions illustrate is that the coterminous United States has experienced periods of severe and long-lasting drought in the western states and also in the more humid East and Mississippi Valley. The drought reconstructions from tree rings document that severe multidecadal drought occurred in the American Southwest during the 13th century, which anthropologists and archeologists suspect profoundly affected Pueblo society. Tree ring drought reconstructions also document severe drought during the 14th, 15th, and 16th centuries in the central and lower Mississippi Valley, possibly contributing to the disintegration of societies in that region.[49]

More recently, a combination of tree ring reconstructions and other proxy data, historical accounts, and some early instrumental records identify three periods of severe drought in the 19th century: 1856-1865 (the "Civil War drought"), 1870-1877, and 1890-1896.[50] The 1856-1865 drought, centered on the Great Plains and Southwest, was the most severe drought to strike the region over the last two centuries, according to one study.[51] The 1890-1896 drought coincided with a period in U.S. history of federal encouragement of large-scale efforts to irrigate the relatively arid western states under authority of the Carey Act.[52] Congressional debate also occurred over a much larger federal role in western states irrigation, which led to the Reclamation Act of 1902.

In the 20th century, the 1930s "Dust Bowl" drought and the 1950s Southwest drought are commonly cited as the two most severe multiyear droughts in the United States.[53] (The 1987-1989 drought was also widespread and severe, mainly affecting the Great Plains but also instigating extensive western forest fires, including the widespread Yellowstone fire of 1988.) According to several studies, however, the 19th and 20th century severe droughts occurred during a regime of relatively less arid conditions compared to the average aridity in the American West during the 900 to 1300 A.D. megadroughts. One study indicates that the drought record from 900 to 1300 A.D. shows similar variability—drought periods followed by wetter periods—compared to today, but the average climate conditions were much drier and led to more severe droughts.[54]

---

[47] Cook et al., 2007.

[48] Proxies are indirect measurements typically used where direct measurements are unavailable. Tree rings can be used as a proxy for measuring dryness and drought. Similarly, ice cores from glaciers and polar caps can be used as proxies for measuring atmospheric temperatures and carbon dioxide concentrations from thousands of years ago.

[49] Cook et al., 2007.

[50] Herweiger et al., 2006.

[51] Ibid.

[52] The Carey Act, signed into law on August 18, 1894 (Chapter 301, Section 4, 28 Stat. 422), initially made available up to 1 million acres of federal land in each state, provided that the state met several requirements for the eventual development of water resources for reclamation. Some observers have suggested that the failure of the Carey Act to foster irrigation projects in all the land made available, compounded in part by the 1890-1896 drought, led to the Reclamation Act of 1902 and the emergence of the Bureau of Reclamation in the 20th century. (See Marc Reisner, *Cadillac Desert* (New York, New York, Penguin Books, 1986)).

[53] Fye, F., D.W. Stahle, and E.R. Cook, "Paleoclimate analogs to twentieth century moisture regimes across the United States," *Bulletin of the American Meteorological Society*, 2003, vol. 84, pp. 901-909.

[54] For example, one report showed that 42% of the area studied in the American West was affected by drought during (continued...)

Responding to and Planning for Drought

Several recent droughts were severe enough to trigger federal responses. When a drought is declared by the U.S. President or by a state governor for a locality or region of the United States, it sets in motion a series of alerts, recommendations, activities, and possible restrictions at the local, regional, or state level, depending on the drought length and severity. Ultimately, a multi-year severe drought could initiate a federal response and transfer of federal dollars to the affected area.

Before drought severity reaches a level triggering a federal response, many states take action. For example, the governor of Alabama issued a drought declaration on March 21, 2008, placing the 10 northernmost counties under an emergency drought declaration level, in accordance with the draft Alabama Drought Management Plan.[55] The emergency drought declaration level for Alabama is its most extreme category of drought. According to Alabama's plan, declaring drought does not "automatically invoke a required response from the various categories of water users;"[56] however, upon confirmation of a drought emergency, the governor's office may issue "public statements that a drought emergency exists, disaster declarations, and the appropriate implementation of water conservation and drought emergency ordinances."[57] The National Drought Mitigation Center posts online copies of drought management, mitigation, or response plans for states and localities, nationwide.[58] The California and Texas governors also have in recent years issued state drought emergency declarations triggering state drought assistance. Some states have also instituted water banks and water transfer mechanisms to deal with water supply shortages (e.g., California, Idaho, and Texas).

Federal Aid

If the effects of a drought overwhelm state or local resources, the President, at the request of the state governor, is authorized under the Stafford Act (42 U.S.C. 5121 et seq.) to issue major disaster or emergency declarations that result in the distribution of federal aid to affected parties.[59] On October 20, 2007, the governor of Georgia requested a presidential drought disaster declaration because of prolonged exceptional drought conditions existing in the northern third of the state.[60] However, no such presidential declaration occurred in response to the request from Georgia. The last presidential drought or water shortage disaster declaration in the continental United States was for New Jersey in 1980. More recent drought declarations have been issued for U.S. territories in the Pacific.

(...continued)

the years 900 to 1300, versus 30% between 1900 and 2003, a 29% reduction in the average area affected by drought between the two periods. See Cook et al., 2007.

[55] For more information, see http://www.adeca.alabama.gov/Office%20of%20Water%20Resources/ Document%20Library/20080321%20-%20DroughtAdvisoryMap_Final.pdf.

[56] Alabama Drought Management Plan, p. 7.

[57] Ibid., p. 8.

[58] For more information, see http://drought.unl.edu/Planning/PlanningInfobyState.aspx.

[59] For more information about the Stafford Act, see CRS Report RL33053, *Federal Stafford Act Disaster Assistance Presidential Declarations, Eligible Activities, and Funding*, by Francis X. McCarthy; and CRS Report R41981, *Congressional Primer on Major Disasters and Emergencies*, by Francis X. McCarthy and Jared T. Brown.

[60] See http://www.fema.gov/news/disasters.fema.

More frequently, a state governor requests drought disaster assistance through the U.S. Secretary of Agriculture, who can declare an agricultural disaster as a result of drought and make available low-interest loans and other emergency assistance through various U.S. Department of Agriculture (USDA) programs.[61] For example, on January 4, 2012, USDA designated 40 counties in Texas as primary natural disaster areas due to losses caused by drought, excessive heat, high winds, and wildfires.[62] During the 2011 drought, USDA designated 213 counties in Texas as primary natural disaster areas on June 27, 2011, when 90% of the state was experiencing extreme drought conditions.[63] The U.S. Army Corps of Engineers and the U.S. Bureau of Reclamation also have limited drought emergency authorities and funding (e.g., the Reclamation States Emergency Drought Act, as amended, 43 U.S.C. 2211 *et seq.*).

Under current U.S. farm policy, financial losses caused by drought and other natural disasters are mitigated primarily through the federal crop insurance program (administered by the U.S. Department of Agriculture's Risk Management Agency). From 2000 to 2011, the federal contribution to the crop insurance program averaged about $4.6 billion per year, mostly in the form of a premium subsidy and reimbursements to private insurance companies. Since the severe drought of 1988 and until passage of the 2008 farm bill (P.L. 110-246) , Congress regularly made supplemental financial assistance available to farmers and ranchers, primarily in the form of crop disaster payments and emergency livestock assistance. Crop disaster payments, paid to any producer who experienced a major crop loss caused by a natural disaster, totaled $22.34 billion from FY1989 to FY2009. More recently, under the 2008 farm bill (P.L. 110-246), Congress authorized a $3.8 billion trust fund to cover the cost of making agricultural disaster assistance available on an ongoing basis over four years (FY2008-FY2011).[64] Among the authorized programs, the Livestock Forage Disaster Program (LFP) assists ranchers who graze livestock on drought-affected pastureland or grazing land. As of early May 2012, payments under LFP totaled more than $500 million for losses through September 2011.

Federal Facilities and Drought

Even absent federal drought disaster declarations, sustained hydrological drought can affect operations of federally managed reservoirs, dams, locks, hydroelectric facilities, and other components of the nation's water infrastructure. As discussed above, the 2007-2008 Southeast drought directly affected how the Corps manages its facilities in the ACF basin (see box on "Federal Reservoir Operations During Southeast Droughts"). Similarly, drought conditions in California from 2007 to 2009, coupled with declining fish species, resulted in operational changes to Reclamation facilities, including significantly reduced water deliveries to Central Valley

---

[61] For more information, see CRS Report RS21212, *Agricultural Disaster Assistance*, by Dennis A. Shields and Ralph M. Chite. See also CRS Report RL34207, *Crop Insurance and Disaster Assistance in the 2008 Farm Bill*, by Ralph M. Chite and Dennis A. Shields.

[62] U.S. Department of Agriculture, Farm Service Agency News Release, January 4, 2012, http://www.fsa.usda.gov/ FSA/newsReleases?area=newsroom&subject=landing&topic=edn&newstype=ednewsrel&type=detail&item= ed_20120104_rel_0003.html.

[63] U.S. Department of Agriculture, Farm Service Agency News Release, June 27, 2011, http://www.fsa.usda.gov/FSA/ newsReleases?area=newsroom&subject=landing&topic=edn&newstype=ednewsrel&type=detail&item= ed_20110628_rel_0061.html.

[64] The causes of crop loss can vary dramatically from year to year, although drought is one of the most common, if not the most common, cause of crop loss. See CRS Report RS21212, *Agricultural Disaster Assistance*, by Dennis A. Shields and Ralph M. Chite, and CRS Report RL31095, *Emergency Funding for Agriculture A Brief History of Supplemental Appropriations, FY1989-FY2012*, by Ralph M. Chite for more information.

Project contractors, as well as to California's State Water Project (SWP) contractors. Reclamation, whose facilities currently serve over 31 million people in the West and deliver a total of nearly 30 million acre-feet of water[65] annually, faces operational challenges because of conflicts among its water users during drought in states it serves.[66]

Federal Reservoir Operations During Southeast Droughts

An example of hydrological drought was the 2007-2008 drought in the southeastern United States. A persistent severe drought in the region, beginning with below-average rainfall in spring 2006, exacerbated an ongoing interstate dispute involving Alabama, Florida, and Georgia over water sharing in the Apalachicola-Chattahoochee-Flint (ACF) river system. During the drought, Atlanta's municipal and industrial water users in the upper basin were concerned over the potential loss of their principal water supply, Lake Lanier, a surface water reservoir behind a U.S. Army Corps of Engineers operated dam. Their concern resulted from the decision by the Corps to draw down Lake Lanier in the fall of 2007. The Corps drew down the reservoir to maintain minimum flows in the lower basin Apalachicola River to support species protection, energy production (e.g., power plant coo ing), and lower basin municipal withdrawals.[67]

The ACF tri-state conflict continues into 2012, and drought conditions have returned to the basin. As of June 2012, the Southeast was experiencing widespread drought, with extreme and exceptional drought in southern Georgia and the northern Florida peninsula. (See **Figure** 1.) Streamflows in the basin in the spring of 2012 were in the lowest quintile on record. Consequently, total inflows into the Corps' ACF reservoirs were below 50% of normal from January to May 2012. As a result, reservoir storage levels are below normal. In May 2012 the Corps shifted its ACF operations to provide only minimum flows to meet water supply, water quality, and environmental needs, thus attempting to store more in its reservoirs. This operation level does not support navigation and only minimal hydropower demands.

During and following the 2007-2008 drought, additional actions at the state level to manage water demand during droughts were used and considered. To what extent similar activities will be implemented or necessary again revives the policy questions of what actions should be taken by whom and when in a shared basin in order to adapt to the dry conditions.

Source: NOAA, National Weather Service, Southeast River Forecast Center, *When Did the Drought Begin, a Focus on the North Georgia and Atlanta Areas,* Nov. 16, 2007; National Integrated Drought Information System, *Southeast US Pilot for Apalachicola-Flint-Chattahoochee River Basin,* June 5, 2012; U.S. Army Corps of Engineers, *Average Daily Inflow to Lakes by Month,* Mobile, AL, June 12, 2012, http://water.sam.usace.army.mil/loclsumm.htm.

Severe drought conditions in 2001 in the Klamath River basin, on the Oregon-California border, exacerbated competition for scarce water resources among farmers, Indian tribes, commercial and sport fishermen, other recreationists, federal wildlife refuge managers, environmental groups, and state, local, and tribal governments. Reclamation's decision in April 2001 to withhold water from farmers for instream flows for three fish species listed as endangered or threatened under the Endangered Species Act sparked congressional debate that continues today. The Klamath basin

---

[65] One acre-foot is enough water to cover one acre of land one foot deep. An acre-foot is equivalent to 325,851 gallons. For more information about federal water supply programs, see CRS Report RL30478, *Federally Supported Water Supply and Wastewater Treatment Programs,* coordinated by Claudia Copeland and others.

[66] Reclamation is a central player in water resource management in the West, and a devastating drought at the end of the 19th century was probably one of the many factors that led to the 1902 Reclamation Act that launched the federal reclamation effort and Reclamation itself. See Marc Reisner, *Cadillac Desert* (New York: Penguin, 1986), pp. 108-109. Other research suggests that the failures of some late 19th century private irrigation projects, undertaken following passage of the Carey Act (see footnote 52), may have occurred in part due to drought conditions.

[67] For more information on the ACF 2007-2008 drought and tri-state conflict, see CRS Report RL34326, *Apalachicola-Chattahoochee-Flint (ACF) Drought Federal Water Management Issues,* coordinated by Nicole T. Carter; and CRS Report RL34440, *Apalachicola-Chattahoochee-Flint Drought Species and Ecosystem Management,* by M. Lynne Corn, Kristina Alexander, and Eugene H. Buck.

---

again experienced drought conditions in 2010 and again is experiencing a lower than average water year for 2012. Project water flows to Klamath refuges were halted from December 2011 through March 2012. Dry conditions contributed to a cholera outbreak among migrating birds during this time, resulting in the death of thousands of birds that visit the refuges. However, early spring precipitation improved hydrological conditions such that Reclamation projects full irrigation deliveries for 2012.[68]

The droughts in California, the Southeast, and the Klamath River basin underscore an underlying difficulty of managing federal reservoirs to meet multipurpose water needs. In the future, the United States might face severe and sustained periods of drought not experienced in the 20th century. If so, disputes over federal infrastructure management like those in California, the ACF basin, and Klamath River basin may increasingly determine short-term actions by Reclamation and the Corps, and result in long-term consequences for congressional oversight and funding.

Drought Forecasts for the United States

Predicting the severity and duration of severe drought over a specific region of the country is not yet possible more than a few months in advance because of the many factors that influence drought. Nevertheless, some modeling studies suggest that a transition to a more arid average climate in the American West, perhaps similar to conditions in precolonial North America, may be underway.[69] Some studies have suggested that human influences on climate, caused by emissions of greenhouse gases, may be responsible for a drying trend.[70] Whether future greenhouse gas-driven warming can be linked to La Niña-like conditions, or other phenomena related to the El Niño-Southern Oscillation, is unclear.

A likely consequence of higher temperatures in the West would be higher evapotranspiration, reduced precipitation, and decreased spring runoff.[71] These impacts would result from an "acceleration" of the hydrologic cycle, due to increased warming of the atmosphere, which in turn increases the amount of water held in the atmosphere.[72] A possible consequence is more frequent, and perhaps more severe, droughts and floods. However, these changes are likely not to occur evenly across the United States. Observations of water-related changes over the last century suggest that runoff and streamflow in the Colorado and Columbia River basins has been decreasing, along with the amount of ice in mountain glaciers in the West, and the amount of annual precipitation in the Southwest.[73] Yet the understanding of hydrologic extremes, such as drought, is confounded by other effects such as land cover changes, the operation of dams,

---

[68] U.S. Bureau of Reclamation, *Klamath Project 2012 Operations Plan*, April 6, 2012, p. 5, http://www.usbr.gov/mp/kbao/docs/summer_operations.pdf.

[69] Richard Seager et al., "Model projections of an imminent transition to a more arid climate in southwestern North America," *Science*, vol. 316 (May 25, 2007), pp. 1181-1184.

[70] Tim P. Barnett, et al., "Human-induced changes in the hydrology of the western United States," *Science*, vol. 319 (February 22, 2008), pp. 1080-1082.

[71] Research results are emerging, however, that suggest that local and regional patterns of precipitation may be variable, and parts of a region or a state could receive higher precipitation than the current average, even if the overall trend over the broader area is towards less precipitation. See K. T. Redmond, "Climate Change in the Western United States: Projections and Observations," *Eos Trans. AGU*, 90(52), Fall Meet. Suppl., Abstract U11D-02, 2009.

[72] National Research Council, Committee on Hydrologic Science, *Global Change and Extreme Hydrology Testing Conventional Wisdom*, Washington, D.C., 2011, p. 3.

[73] Ibid., p. 7.

---

irrigation works, extraction of groundwater, and other engineered changes. Forecasting drought conditions at the regional scale, for example for river basins or smaller, is difficult because current climate models are less robust and have higher uncertainty at smaller scales.[74] (For example, see box below on the Colorado River's Lake Mead.)

Even though forecasting drought at the regional scale is difficult, understanding potential changes in long-term trends is important for water managers at all levels—federal, state, local, and tribal. Water project operations and state water allocations are typically based on past long-term hydrological trends; significant deviations from such trends may result in difficult challenges for water managers and water users alike.[75] An example of such a dilemma can be observed in the Colorado River basin.

Colorado River's Lake Mead

A 2008 study asserted that water storage in Lake Mead has a 50% probability by 2021 to "run dry" and a 10% chance by 2014 to drop below levels needed to provide hydroelectric power under current c imate conditions and without changes to water allocation in the basin. This study raised awareness of the vulnerability of western water systems but drew criticism that global climate models are insufficient to forecast climate change effects at the regional scale. Some western water officials were especially critical of the report's assertions. One explained that Reclamation and other agencies had recently developed new criteria for the allocation of Colorado River water in times of shortages (shortage criteria), including drought, and commented that the likelihood that Lake Mead would run dry was "absurd." The study was based on predictions of future warming in the West without increased precipitation.

In a 2009 follow-up study, the same authors acknowledged that the ability of the Colorado River system to mitigate drought could be managed if the users found a way to reduce average deliveries, thereby maintaining water levels in Lake Mead and Lake Powell at consistently higher elevations. Maintaining higher water levels would increase the capacity of the Colorado River system to buffer itself against low precipitation years. Even so, the authors noted, global climate models are in broad agreement that the southwestern United States is likely to become warmer and more arid, especially in the Colorado River drainage basin. In addition, paleoc imate studies suggest that the 20th century was the wettest or second-wettest century for at least 500 years and possibly over the past 1,200 years. Notwithstanding climate change, the paleoclimate data suggest that average future precipitation in the Colorado River basin is unlikely to match what hydrologists believe were relatively wet 20th-century levels.

Sources: Tim P. Barnett and David W. Pierce, "When Will Lake Mead Go Dry?" *Water Resources Research,* vol. 44 (March 29, 2008), p. W03201, DOI:10.1029/2007WR006704; Felicity Barringer, "Lake Mead could be within a few years of going dry, study finds," *New York Times* (Feb. 13, 2008); Jenny Dennis, "Stunned Scientists: 'When Will Lake Mead Go Dry?'" *Rim Country Gazette* (Feb. 28, 2008), quoting Larry Dozier, Central Arizona Project deputy general manager; Timothy P. Barnett and David W. Pierce, "Sustainable Water Deliveries from the Colorado River in a Changing Climate," *Proceedings of the National Academy of Sciences,* vol. 106, no. 18 (May 6, 2009).

Conditions in the Colorado River basin over the last decade, including recent low reservoir levels in Lake Mead and low flows in the Upper Basin, raise the issue of what is the baseline for average hydrologic cycles now and in the future. The allocation of Colorado River water supplies was agreed upon by lower and upper basin states in the early part of the 20th century based on hydrologic data from what scientists now know was a relatively wet period in the history of the Colorado River basin.[76] If long-term reduced runoff predictions for the basin are borne out (see

---

[74] Ibid., p. 9.

[75] P.C.D. Milly et al., "Stationarity Is Dead: Whither Water Management?," *Science,* vol. 319 (February 4, 2008), p. 574.

[76] The Colorado River basin is somewhat unusual in that the Secretary of the Interior acts as water "master" for the river, and apportionment of water supplies among the basin states is done in accordance with the Colorado River Compact and a body of law known as the "Law of the River." For more information on the Law of the River, see (continued...)

---

box above on Colorado River's Lake Mead), then water allocation policies for regions like the Colorado River basin may need to be revisited.[77] In the meantime, Colorado River basin states have negotiated "shortage criteria" and "interim guidelines" for managing Colorado River water supplies during times of shortages.[78]

Policy Challenges

Severe drought can exacerbate water competition, cause significant economic harm, and affect nearly all areas of the country. Nonetheless, several key factors make comprehensive drought policy at the national level a challenge, including:

- the "creeping" nature of drought;

- split federal and non-federal drought response and management responsibilities;

- a patchwork of federal programs and oversight with little coordination; and

- differences in regional conditions and drought risk in terms of the drought hazard, vulnerability, and potential consequences.

Drought conditions often develop slowly and are not easily identified initially. Consequently, drought declarations are made well after onset—typically once impacts are felt. This situation makes it difficult to mitigate or prevent drought impacts. Further, even though drought generally is continuously occurring somewhere in the United States, the unpredictability of its location, duration, and severity complicates preparation for implementation of responses.

When severe meteorological drought affects a region, the supply of available water often shrinks before use is reduced. Adjusting down the use of water as drought persists and supplies shrink can be difficult. Actually, droughts can increase demand on water supplies (e.g., lower soil moisture results in increased demand for irrigation and landscape watering). The flexibility of existing water access and use arrangements limit the scope and speed of some drought responses. Federal, state, and local authorities make water resource decisions within the context of multiple and often conflicting laws and objectives, competing legal decisions, and entrenched institutional mechanisms, including century-old water rights and long-standing contractual obligations (i.e., long-term water delivery and power contracts). Typically, how access to and competition for water is managed (e.g., permitting of water withdrawals) and how reductions in water supply are managed (e.g., shared reductions under a riparian system of water rights versus reductions based on the priority in time of a water right) is determined by state law and at times through interstate compacts. Additionally, state and local laws can determine how easily water can be transferred

---

(...continued)

http://www.usbr.gov/lc/region/g1000/lawofrvr.html.

[77] Tim P. Barnett and David W. Pierce, "When Will Lake Mead Go Dry?" *Water Resources Research*, vol. 44 (March 29, 2008), p. W03201, DOI:10.1029/2007WR006704. Reservoir storage in the Colorado River basin has increased by more than 8 million acre-feet since 2005. As of April 3, 2012, reservoir storage in the basin was nearly 63% of capacity. Hydropower production has continued under 2007 "interim guidelines" for managing water shortages in the Lower Colorado River basin.

[78] For more information on 2012 operations, see http://www.usbr.gov/uc/water/crsp/studies/24Month_03.pdf, accessed May 2, 2012. CRS has not determined to what degree recent scenarios are similar to those considered in studies supporting the new shortage criteria for Colorado River water allocations under the Colorado River Compact.

---

among users. These access, reduction, and transfer arrangements can significantly affect the behavior, incentives, and opportunities available to water users during droughts. Fundamental changes to the access, reduction, and transfer arrangements are largely outside of the realm of federal action, and are largely determined by each state.

A mismatch between supply and demand during droughts underscores the responsibility of stakeholders to anticipate the influence of drought and plan and act accordingly. The federal government has several drought monitoring and response programs. While drought planning and mitigation responsibilities lie largely at the state and local level, the federal government also provides some drought planning assistance. Additionally, the federal government often provides emergency funding for drought relief that is primarily aimed at easing the economic impacts. The National Drought Commission and others have noted, however, that federal relief programs and emergency funding provide little incentive for state and local planning and drought mitigation. A policy issue particularly relevant to state and local decision makers is the role and types of demand management tools to employ during a drought (e.g., lawn watering restrictions, incentives to curtail irrigation during droughts, scarcity pricing). How a state distributes and administers its waters among competing uses can affect what drought response tools are available to it and to water users.

Australia's Drought Experience: Water Markets as Drought Management

Australia experienced a historic drought from 1997 to 2009, known as the Millennium Drought. The drought tested a preexisting multi-pronged national water reform initiative; one aspect of the reform was the development of water markets. To develop water markets, the initiative had promoted reform of state law to clarify the property right associated with a water right and facilitated the means to buy and sell perpetual water rights and short-term allocations in basins that were fully allocated. Water trade increased significantly during the later years of the drought as allocations fell and markets matured. Allocations in some sub-basins during the worst of the drought reached as low as 20% of a full allocation. While gross domestic production dropped by $2 billion-$3 billion in Australia's most significant agricultural basin during each of the worst drought years, the ability to trade water is estimated to have reduced losses by roughly $1 billion during each drought year. The market's ability to move scarce water to uses with higher economic value is credited with assisting Australia's rural economy to ride out the drought as well as it did by getting more value per unit of water used. For example, some dairy farmers sold their water rights and purchased fodder, rather than growing it themselves. Agricultural businesses increasingly used buying and selling in the water market as a coping mechanism as the drought persisted. With water availability high in many basins since 2009, market water prices have fallen, and rice and cotton production, which had declined during the drought, have picked back up.

Water markets were not established in Australia without controversy and criticism. While not solely responsible, water rights trading contributed to trends producing significant economic adjustment, particularly in rural agricultural communities. Nonetheless, contemplating the consequences for Australia, especially its agricultural communities and businesses, of such a severe drought under a less flexible water rights regime has increased internal support for the use and further improvement of water markets.

The broader water reform initiative produced some disappointments, as well as successes. The broader reform is criticized for falling short of achieving ecologically sustainable levels of surface water withdrawals. Consequently, the recent discourse about the next steps in Australian water policy has focused on how to establish sustainable levels of withdrawals that can maintain ecosystems and support regional economies and how to cost-effectively secure the water for the environment. Australia's government uses the water markets to transition water out of existing uses for use in meeting environmental flow goals; to date, the Australian government's purchase of water rights for the environment using the market has been less expensive than obtaining the water through infrastructure efficiency improvements.

Source: National Water Commission (Australia), *The Impacts of Water Trading in the Southern Murray-Darling Basin Between 2006-07 and 2010-11*, April 2012.

A further challenge is lack of a cohesive national drought policy at the federal level, and lack of a lead agency coordinating federal programs. Rather, several federal programs have been developed over the years, often in response to specific droughts. Additionally, occasional widespread economic effects have prompted creation of several federal relief programs. These programs are overseen by different congressional committees. Whether this fragmentation results in duplication, waste, and gaps, or whether it reflects the complexity of preparing and responding to drought and the different responses needed by a wide range of stakeholders (e.g., irrigated agriculture, dry land farming, municipal water utilities) is part of the debate about how to proceed with cost-effective management of the nation's drought risk and who bears the consequences of drought. (See box above for an example of how water access and transfer arrangements played a significant role in shaping Australia's drought resilience and adaptation.)

Legislative Action

Congress has long recognized the lack of coordinated drought planning and mitigation activities among federal agencies and the predominance of a crisis management approach to dealing with drought. Over the last 15 years, legislative action has focused on the question of whether there is a need for a national drought policy. For example, in 1998, Congress passed the National Drought Policy Act (P.L. 105-199), which created a National Drought Policy Commission. In 2000, the commission submitted to Congress a comprehensive report that included policy recommendations. Congress has considered recommendations from the commission's 2000 report; however, to date, it has enacted only one part of the recommendations (the National Integrated Drought Information System, discussed below). Congress also considered, but did not enact, legislation creating a National Drought Council during deliberations on the 2008 farm bill. Both the commission findings and the proposed council are discussed below.

The National Drought Policy Act of 1998

In passing the National Drought Policy Act of 1998, Congress found that "at the Federal level, even though historically there have been frequent, significant droughts of national consequences, drought is addressed mainly through special legislation and ad hoc action rather than through a systematic and permanent process as occurs with other natural disasters."[79] Further, Congress found an increasing need at the federal level to emphasize preparedness, mitigation, and risk management. Those findings are consistent with a recognition of the inevitability, albeit unpredictability, of severe drought occurring.

The act created the National Drought Policy Commission, and required the commission to conduct a study and submit a report to Congress on:

- what is needed to respond to drought emergencies;

- what federal laws and programs address drought;

- what are the pertinent state, tribal, and local laws; and

- how various needs, laws, and programs can be better integrated while recognizing the primacy of states to control water through state law.

---

[79] The National Drought Policy Act of 1998, P.L. 105-199 (42 U.S.C. 5121 note).

In May 2000, the commission submitted its report,[80] which included 29 specific recommendations to achieve the goals of national drought policy, including the establishment of a National Drought Council. (The **Appendix** of this report lists the five goals in the commission's report.) As background for its recommendations, the commission noted the patchwork nature of drought programs, and that despite a major federal role in responding to drought, no single federal agency leads or coordinates drought programs—instead, the federal role is more of "crisis management."[81] Most of the specific recommendations were targeted at the President and federal agencies, coupled with calls for Congress to fund drought-related activities in support of the recommendations. An overarching recommendation was for Congress to pass a National Drought Preparedness Act to implement the commission's recommendations.

National Drought Preparedness Legislation and the 2008 Farm Bill

National Drought Preparedness Act bills were introduced in 2002 (107th Congress), 2003 (108th Congress), and 2005 (109th Congress), but were not enacted. Similar stand-alone legislation was introduced in the 110th Congress; however, the House-passed version of H.R. 2419, the Farm, Nutrition, and Bioenergy Act of 2008 (also known as the 2008 farm bill), contained a section creating a National Drought Council. This section of the 2008 farm bill would have charged the council with creating a national drought policy action plan, which would have incorporated many of the components recommended in the commission's report; however, it was not included in the conference agreement. Although the Senate version of H.R. 2419 did not contain a similar section, the Senate bill authorized permanent disaster payments in hopes of precluding the need for ad hoc disaster payments. The conference agreement on the 2008 farm bill (P.L. 110-246, enacted June 18, 2008) included a new $3.8 billion trust fund to cover the cost of making agricultural disaster assistance available on an ongoing basis over the following four years. The assistance was available for disasters occurring on or before September 30, 2011, and has since expired. The Senate Agriculture Committee version of the 2012 farm bill would authorize four of the five disaster programs that received funding under the authority of the 2008 farm bill.[82]

National Integrated Drought Information System

Although Congress has not enacted comprehensive national drought preparedness legislation, it acted on the second of five commission goals by passing the National Integrated Drought Information System (NIDIS) Act of 2006 (P.L. 109-430). That goal called for enhanced observation networks, monitoring, prediction, and information delivery of drought information. P.L. 109-430 established NIDIS within the National Oceanic and Atmospheric Administration (NOAA) to improve drought monitoring and forecasting abilities.[83]

---

[80] Available at http://govinfo.library.unt.edu/drought/finalreport/fullreport/ndpcfullreportcovers/ndpcreportcontents.htm.

[81] Ibid., p. 1.

[82] See CRS Report R42040, *Farm Safety Net Proposals in the 112th Congress*, by Dennis A. Shields and Randy Schnepf.

[83] NOAA allocated $12 1 million for NIDIS in FY2012. For more information about NIDIS, see http://www.drought.gov.

Conclusion

Drought is a natural hazard with potentially significant economic, social, and ecological consequences. History suggests that severe and extended droughts are inevitable and part of natural climate cycles. Drought has for centuries shaped the societies of North America and will continue to do so into the future. Current understanding is that the physical conditions causing drought in the United States are linked to sea surface temperatures in the tropical Pacific Ocean. For example, the 2011 severe drought in Texas is thought to be linked to La Niña conditions in the Pacific Ocean. Increasingly, studies are projecting the long-term role that droughts may play in regional climate patterns. Nonetheless, available technology and science remains limited to forecasting specific drought beyond a few months in advance for a region. The prospect of extended droughts and more arid baseline conditions in parts of the United States represents a challenge to existing public policy responses for preparing and responding to drought, and to federal water resource projects in particular, because their construction was based largely on 19th- and 20th-century hydrologic conditions.

Over time, Congress has created various drought programs, often in response to specific droughts and authored by different committees. Crafting a broad drought policy that might encompass the jurisdiction of many different congressional committees is often difficult. Additionally, although many water allocation and other water management responsibilities largely lie at the state or local level, localities and individuals often look to the federal government for relief when disasters occur. This is similar to the situation for flood policy, and water policy in general, at the national level. The National Drought Policy Commission recognized these patterns, and they underlie many of its recommendations to Congress.[84] The currently fragmented approach can be costly to national taxpayers; however, it is not certain that increased federal investment (especially vis-à-vis the potential for tailored local and state investment) in drought preparation, mitigation, and improved coordination would produce more economically efficient outcomes.

The overall costs to the federal government as a result of extreme drought, apart from relief to the agricultural sector, are difficult to assess. As discussed above, the operation of the nation's complex federal water infrastructure is affected by drought.

Congress may opt to revisit the commission's recommendations and reevaluate whether current federal practices could be supplemented with actions to coordinate, prepare for, and respond to the unpredictable but inevitable occurrence of drought. Given the daunting task of managing drought, Congress also may consider proposals to manage drought impacts, such as assisting localities, industries, and agriculture with developing or augmenting water supplies. Congress also may move to examine how the two major federal water management agencies, the Corps and Reclamation, plan for and respond to severe drought and account for its impacts.

---

[84] *Infra*, note 52.

Appendix. Excerpt from the 2000 National Drought Policy Commission Report to Congress

The following is an excerpt from the 2000 National Drought Policy Commission Report to Congress: *Preparing for Drought in the 21ˢᵗ Century—A Report of the National Drought Policy Commission.*

Policy Statement

- Favor preparedness over insurance, insurance over relief, and incentives over regulation.

- Set research priorities based on the potential of the research results to reduce drought impacts.

- Coordinate the delivery of federal services through cooperation and collaboration with nonfederal entities.

Goals

Goal 1. Incorporate planning, implementation of plans and proactive mitigation measures, risk management, resource stewardship, environmental considerations, and public education as the key elements of effective national drought policy.

Goal 2. Improve collaboration among scientists and managers to enhance the effectiveness of observation networks, monitoring, prediction, information delivery, and applied research and to foster public understanding of and preparedness for drought.

Goal 3. Develop and incorporate comprehensive insurance and financial strategies into drought preparedness plans.

Goal 4. Maintain a safety net of emergency relief that emphasizes sound stewardship of natural resources and self-help.

Goal 5. Coordinate drought programs and response effectively, efficiently, and in a customer-oriented manner.

Author Contact Information

Peter Folger
Specialist in Energy and Natural Resources Policy
pfolger@crs.loc.gov, 7-1517

Betsy A. Cody
Specialist in Natural Resources Policy
bcody@crs.loc.gov, 7-7229

Nicole T. Carter
Specialist in Natural Resources Policy
ncarter@crs.loc.gov, 7-0854